Too Risky!

By Alison Hawes

Illustrated by
David Shephard

Titles in the Zipwire series:

Who Are You?	David Orme
3Dee	Danny Pearson
Doom Clone	Melanie Joyce
Too Risky!	Alison Hawes
Wanda Darkstar	Jane A C West
Galactic Games	Roger Hurn
Robot Eyes	Jillian Powell
Charlie's Tin	Lynda Gore
Run For Your Life	Jonny Zucker
Changing Rooms	Melanie Joyce

Badger Publishing Limited
Oldmedow Road, Hardwick Industrial Estate,
King's Lynn PE30 4JJ
Telephone: 01553 769209
www.badgerlearning.co.uk

6 8 10 9 7 5

Too Risky! ISBN 978-1-78837-603-7

Text © Alison Hawes 2011
Complete work © Badger Publishing Limited 2021

All rights reserved. No part of this publication may be reproduced, stored in any form or by any means mechanical, electronic, recording or otherwise without the prior permission of the publisher.

The right of Alison Hawes to be identified as author of this Work has been asserted by her in accordance with the Copyright, Designs and Patents Act 1988.

Badger Publishing would like to thank Jonny Zucker for his help in putting this series together.

Commissioning Editor: Sarah Rudd
Editor: Claire Morgan
Typesetting: Adam Wilmott
Illustration: David Shephard
Page 32 illustration: Juliet Breese
Cover design: Shaun Page
Font: OpenDyslexic

Too Risky!

Contents

Chapter 1	5
Chapter 2	9
Chapter 3	14
Chapter 4	18
Chapter 5	22
Chapter 6	25
Questions	30

Chapter 1

Anna lined herself up for the last kick of the match.

The crowd went quiet.

Anna ran at the ball and kicked it high into the air.

It landed just short of the bar.

It was the only kick Anna had missed the entire match.

The final whistle blew and the teams walked off the pitch.

Anna's friend Joe spoke to her as she walked past.

"Never mind, Anna," he said.

Anna was too upset to speak.

Then she saw her team manager.

"Come to my office before you go home, Anna. I need to talk to you," said the manager.

Anna went into the changing room and started to cry.

Chapter 2

Anna got changed and went outside to find Joe.

"I can't go home yet," she said. "The manager wants to see me."

"Ok," said Joe. "Don't look so sad. You had a great game!"

Anna went into the manager's office.

"I wanted to tell you the good news," the manager said. "You've been chosen for the senior team!"

"I can't believe it!" grinned Anna.

Anna couldn't wait to tell Joe.

Anna dashed out of the office and into the street.

She saw Joe across the road.

"Joe!" she yelled. "Wait for me!"

Joe stopped.

He turned to see Anna running straight into the path of a car.

Chapter 3

Anna was thrown high into the air.

She landed in the path of another car.

There was nothing the driver could do.

Anna was trapped under the second car.

She was alive but had been knocked out.

Joe phoned for an ambulance.

Then he phoned Anna's mum and dad.

Anna's mum answered.

"There's been an accident," said Joe. "Anna was hit by a car."

"How bad?" cried Anna's mum.

"It's bad. Really bad," said Joe.

Chapter 4

For days, Anna drifted in and out of sleep.

She couldn't move.

One day, Joe was there.

"I'm glad you're here," Anna said. "There's something I want to tell you."

"What's that?" asked Joe.

"I'm going to play for the senior rugby team!" Anna replied.

Joe started crying.

Joe never cried.

Anna knew something was very wrong.

It was Anna's dad who told her she wouldn't play rugby again.

Anna couldn't believe it at first.

She would spend the rest of her life in a wheelchair.

Chapter 5

It was months before Anna went back to school.

Joe took Anna to watch her old team play rugby.

But it upset Anna.

She missed playing too much.

One day, Joe found something on the internet.

"You have to see this!" he said to Anna.

Anna couldn't believe it.

"What is this?" she asked.

"It's wheelchair rugby," Joe replied.

"It looks brilliant!" said Anna.

Anna watched the players smash their wheelchairs into each other.

"They play it at the sports centre," said Joe. "Do you want to go?"

"Of course I want to go!" laughed Anna.

Chapter 6

On Friday, Anna's mum took her to the sports centre to play wheelchair rugby.

Anna's mum thought it looked too risky but Anna really wanted to try it.

The first time someone crashed into Anna's wheelchair, it took her breath away.

It was very fast and a bit scary.

Anna had never played a game that was so much fun!

The sports centre lent Anna a special sports wheelchair.

She had to get used to it.

Anna got stronger and faster over time.

One day, she was given a place on the team.

Anna couldn't wait to tell her mum and dad.

"Well, it's lucky we got you this then," they grinned.

They brought out a brand new sports wheelchair.

It was just for Anna!

"We can't wait to come and watch you play," said Mum.

Anna was so happy to be on a rugby team again.

Questions

What is Anna's good news at the start of the story? *(page 10)*

Who phones for an ambulance? *(page 16)*

What news does Anna's dad give her? *(page 21)*

What does Joe see on the internet? *(page 23)*

zipwire

Looking for your next read?

Have a look at all the great books in the Zipwire series

badgerlearning.co.uk **@badgerlearning**